Becoming a Pioneer

Becoming a Pioneer

A Book Series

The Month-by-Month Guide
to Double your Business and
Take Over Your Industry in a Year

Bimal Shah

Book 5: Leveraging your Biggest Strengths and Managing Your Weaknesses

Becoming a Pioneer - Book 5

© Copyright 2022 by Bimal Shah

ISBN: 978-1-0878-7423-4 Paperback

ISBN: 978-1-0879-2281-2 Ebook

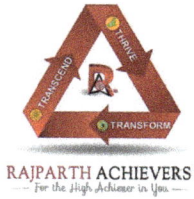

RAJPARTH ACHIEVERS
— For the High Achiever in You —

TheOneYearBreakthrough.com

For more information, email: Bimal@theoneyearbreakthrough.com

Rajparth Achievers, LLC
5550 Glades Road, Suite 500
Boca Raton, FL 33431

WHAT IS THE PIONEER CLUB FOR A BUCK?

- Buy the book for a Buck and you join the club
- Meet and network with other Pioneers
- Walk away with great results at the club meeting
- Complete the exercises in the book
- FREE Tools and Resources
- Win an Invitation to the Mastermind (**$495 Value**)
- Provide a great review on Amazon

https://bit.ly/ThePioneersClub

Connect with Pioneers around the World. Every Month. With the book purchase, you are a member. No strings attached.

Join Me and walk away with personalized insights for you in the monthly Club meeting.

Get Your Free Membership here
https://bit.ly/ThePioneersClub

Learn Exponentially More.

This book is best used in conjunction with its training which allows you to not only leverage your biggest strengths but also strategically and tactically manage your weaknesses to exponentially scale your business in a year.

Get Your Free Video Training at
https://bit.ly/TheStrengthsLeverage

To my wife, Ami, and our daughters, Rajvi, and Parthvi. This book would not have been possible without the efforts of Ami with the editing. Her strength and support are priceless. Also, I am indebted to my daughters for their invaluable insight into the structure and design. My family is everything to me.

I love them with all my heart.

Content

Author's Preface

Making Pioneers! —The What and Why

What is a Pioneer?

A pioneer is unique and different from the rest.

To be a pioneer, you need to be the Only One at something. This book is about breaking all the barriers and obstacles you have in your life, work, habits, and mindset. The purpose of this book is to bring a 10x to a 100x transformation in your perspective about yourself—to assist you in realizing your true potential in a very short time.

Why be a Pioneer?

God has made every human being unique and different. When every human becomes unique and different, the whole world can work in harmony. Becoming a pioneer happens through stages and discoveries. I wrote this book with the intent to create the essential stages and discoveries you will need at each step. Drawing from my own experiences, it builds fresh perspectives that can take your business to the next level.

Editor Ami Shah with Author Bimal Shah

How To Get the Most Out of This Book Series

Go slow. This is a book you do not want to read fast. Write in the margins. Scribble in it, make notes, and use sticky notes. Carry this book with you wherever you go. This is your book and customized manual to help you at least double what you believe you can do in a year.

Even if you answer one question from this book, it will have a positive impact on your life or business. Below are five ways you can make the most out of it:

1. Read first, think second, and then write: Read a sentence or two or a paragraph. Think about it and answer the questions that follow.

2. Go digging: Look up something in your business or your personal life related to the question. And then come back and answer the question.

3. Use Sharp Pencils with an eraser on top: Instead of using pens, please use pencils, as while you are writing your thoughts on the questions, the answers may change in due course.

4. Watch the video before you start reading: In the video, you will get a lot more insights into the book itself. It will walk you through powerful elements to scale.

5. Scan the QR CODE and save the QR CODE link in your Notes on your Smartphone: When you answer a specific question, look up the links listed in the Link Tree. See if there is a resource for the problem you are trying to solve. The Link Tree is very useful. It works like magic; you will find new and amazing things each time you look.

Special Advice for Using This Book
in Uncertain Economic Times

As we all know, the future is questionable. I recommend using this book series in a sequential order to stabilize and speed up your income growth. Follow the advice in the acronym UNCERTAIN:

U-Unique - Discover from each book how to become unique.
Book #5 lists elements to leverage to be unique.

N-New – Apply the different tools and systems taught in book #1, book #9, and book #11. To bring in the new you in record time.

C-Confidence – Use the Confidence Journey tool from book #5. To build daily confidence in your journey.

E-Empathy – Use the Self-Empathy skills from book #10 and book #2 (this one). To deal with uncertainties, biggest pains, or frustrations.

R-Resilience – Lay the foundation for building resilience with a powerful vision in book #1. Apply Book #12 resiliency skills.

T-Transparency – Discover from book #3, book #4, and book #6 how to use good or bad transparency. This is to propel you and your business to the next level.

A-Audacious – From book #1, book #13, and book #6 you will discover how to maintain and chase audacious goals.

I-Implementation – From Book #7 on Sprints and Book #8 on Leadership. Throughout each book in the series, you will become a master implementor.

N-Next Steps – Every single chapter in each book helps you build your customized next steps. There is no way you can't stabilize or grow if you follow all the steps you built by yourself, using this book series.

Special Advice for Using this Book Series
in Prosperous Economic Times

When times are good, you can make them better by using this book series with the acronym AWESOME as follows:

A-Algorithms - In business when there are a lot of opportunities coming your way, you need to apply an algorithm: a one-line business plan. Build your customized scale from algorithms listed in book #4 and book #13.

W-Wins – At the end of every chapter, you celebrate your wins. In book #5 you have the tools that make it a recurring habit.

E-Extra –There is no traffic beside you in the extra mile. In book #12, you will have the systems to drive on no-traffic roads.

S-Surprisers –What to do when your team and customers surprise you. You are bound to get surprised quite often. Discover the best responses in book #1, book #2 (this book), book #3, book #4, and book #10.

O-Omnipresence –Through book #6 and book #3, you will build your systems. Through book #11 you will build your own skill sets. Through book #9 you will build the platforms. In book #10 you will have the systems and tools to automate omnipresence.

M-Multiplication –When times are good, you need systems to multiply. Through Book #1 you will lay the foundation for multiplication. Through Book #7 you will build the skills. Through Book #8 and book #9, you will build the traits for becoming a multiplier and the systems essential for it.

E-Extinguishers –When things are happening like rapid fire, you need a different kind of extinguisher. This is to extinguish the fires and keep up the pace you are moving at. Build your fire extinguishers from book #5.

Introduction

This book is written with the intent to make an immediate positive impact on you, the reader. Hence, there are more questions, with immensely valuable tools, resources, stories, and action steps.

This way you can even answer one question and see a positive impact. I want you to have notes all over this book and that's why I left a lot of spaces for you. I want you to make this book your "own unique book."

There are many self-development and business books out there. But I wrote this one to direct your thinking in a specific way. So, sit back and relax while you read.

There is just one topic in this book that allows you to go deep. It also helps to make a real positive difference in the least amount of time. Even if you spend five minutes reading this book, you will feel the transformation.

What's unique and different about this book is that it is a series you will cherish forever. It has your goals, your plans, your actions, and most of all a system you can use every year.

The system consists of a series of 13 stages. Each last 4 Weeks; you can achieve your 3-year goal in one Year. Besides, I did not want to write anything about something you already knew.

Alongside the questions for you to answer are tools to use. And some practical solutions you can put in place and see great results.

I hope this book will make a positive impact on your life.
For your convenience, I have left you enough space for answering each question. I have noticed many people have bigger handwriting and need more space to write!

Eagerly looking forward to meeting you in Part VI!

Week 1

The Strengths-Confidence Loop

I used to see strength as being physically strong. I was wrong. Now I know that you may see yourself strong in certain areas and weak in certain areas. The reality is that there is a strength-confidence loop that consistently allows everyone to be strong and confident. If you are strong, you are confident and if you are confident, you are strong. That's the strength-confidence loop.

I lost 65 pounds through just diet and exercise, and I have shared those systems in the QR code after this chapter. But the main ingredient was the strength-confidence loop. I built that loop for myself, and magic happened. It took me a while to build it. The loop began with getting clarity on the purpose of losing weight and getting healthy. The purpose was tied to my long-term 25-year vision. This is something that I have shared in Book # 1 of the series. The vision allowed me to connect to other elements that lead to the confidence to build the loop. Once I built, it was a smooth ride with the wind to my back. Now I am not a super guy with muscles and a six-pack, but I feel strong and confident every day with the Strengths-Confidence loop.

Below I will walk you through a series of questions, next steps, action items, thinking tools, and the amazing powerful Confidence Journey that you can use every day to build the strength-confidence loop.

Now, let's look at your strengths and how to strengthen them.

What do strengths mean to you in your life and your business?

Strengths are tasks or actions that an individual can perform at an optimal level and better than others. For example, strengths in your business, are those things that you do, say delivering top-notch services on time, your products are always well packaged, and good customer service, and providing a dream come true experience for your customers that help you get better and consistent results for them as well as your business.

What do you do that drives consistent and great results for your customers?

Think about what your customers always compliment you about, where they got the most value, and what makes you unique and different. This will help you answer the above question.

There is a book called "The Strengths Finder 2.0" by Tom Rath and I have personally used the assessment to find my strengths. It has been very useful in determining my strengths and how to leverage them. My strengths discovered through that were Achiever, Relator, Focus, Responsible, and Maximizer. They have been useful to me in my journey to success throughout my life. You should try it.

If you have figured out your strengths and you know them clearly, I applaud you. A lot of people haven't taken out the time to figure out what their strengths are. If not, you can use "The Strengths Finder 2.0 to begin. Regardless of whether you have figured out your strengths or not, you can use the questions below to either build or improve your strengths.

What is the single most activity that you do that you can do all day long that fascinates you, motivates you, and you get energy by working on it instead of getting tired from it?

_____

_____

_____

_____

_____

_____

_____

_____

What are the top five unique character traits of you that you continue to display consistently in your daily actions and interactions and your talks that deliver positive outcomes?

1._____

_____

2._____

_____

3._____

_____

4._____

_____

5._____

_____

What is the optimal way or strategy to apply each of these traits in your business to improve the results you can deliver to your customers and yourself in your business?

1._____

_____

2._____

_____

3._____

_____

4._____

_____

5._____

_____

Now let's revisit the results you wrote earlier and improve them. What would be the improved results you would be able to achieve in your business because of the above strategies?

_____

_____

_____

_____

_____

_____

Now that you have some idea of your unique strengths, it is essential to integrate them into your skills, knowledge, capabilities, proficiencies, and talents.

What skills, capabilities, knowledge, proficiencies, and talents can you incorporate your unique strengths into?

_____

_____

_____

_____

_____

_____

_____

_____

As an entrepreneur, you should not only use your strengths in your personal life but also your business. You should now identify your current business strengths.

Examples of business strengths you could have been, excellent customer service, and personal relationships with customers, this will help you acquire and retain customers, which is necessary for the longevity of your business. Let's do a self-reflection exercise here, making a list of your top 10 business strengths.

Sit down in a quiet corner and think of instances where you pushed through no matter the odds, and you were successful. Think of situations where others had given up or saw no way out, you could find a way to come out of it successfully. Think of the traits that helped you do the same. Those are the traits that will improve or enhance the business strengths or even discover hidden business strengths that you haven't discovered yet. Also, have your teammates do this too.

1._____

2._____

3._____

4._____

5._____

6._____

7._____

8._____

9._____

10._____

Some examples of strengths are, innovation, adaptability, pivoting, learning, flawless execution, ideation, innovation, creativity, evaluation, analytical reasoning, guidance, direction, editing, delegation, managing, motivation, marketing, product development, research, strategy, team building, training, and so on. They are numerous, so you and your team-mates should be able to come up with 10.

Kudos on carrying out this task. If you haven't, please take your time to go back and do it. As it will help you in making crucial decisions about your company.

As an entrepreneur, you are a leader, you are an innovator, you are an executor, a strategist, a financier, a manager and so much more. An entrepreneur wears so many hats. The most important hat you wear is that of a results leader to lead yourself and others for better results consistently.

To be an effective results leader, what are the five most essential strengths that you need to have?

1._____

_____

2._____

_____

3._____

_____

4._____

_____

5._____

_____

Now that you have identified what strengths you need to have as a results leader, what are the top five strengths your business needs to have to be a results leader in the industry?

1._____

_____

2._____

_____

3._____

_____

4._____

_____

5._____

_____

Take these strengths and convert those into the top 10 action items for your business. The biggest gap that exists in businesses today is execution and getting it done. One of the main reasons it exists is because of the approach to execution being reactive than proactive. Therefore, I have developed a tool called "The Implementation Guarantor™" that does proactive execution. Instead of just making a list of things or actions to do, if you utilize the tool on the next page, you will see a 10 to 100 times more effective outcome. This is an important tool that you want to use for any type of action you want to take, or you want your team members to take in your business that requires oversight, strategy, and follow-through.

The Implementation Guarantor™

Prepared For_____

Start Date: _____   End Date: _____

Results that you want to Achieve	Who?	What Specific Action needs to be taken to achieve that result?	By When?	Review Date?

The Implementation Guarantor™

Prepared For_____

Start Date _____   End Date _____

What are the obstacles, opposition or challenges you faced?	What Solutions will you implement to overcome those?	Result Achieved and By When

The second reason that the execution gap is present is because of how the action items are communicated. It is very essential on learning how to effectively communicate what needs to be done. That is a huge impact on what gets done and what doesn't get done.

Can you rightly communicate what needs to get done and by when?
❏ Y ❏ N

If yes, that's great. If not, you need to start working on your communication skills, you can go to https://bit.ly/BetterCommunicationSkills to help you improve your ability to convey your thoughts properly.

What are your top 5 strengths relating to your optimal and effective communication?

1._____
_____

2._____
_____

3._____
_____

4._____
_____

5._____
_____

To be a results leader, some of the ways you can optimally communicate are active and genuine listening, tone, volume, and clarity when communicating, sharing feedback, and getting buy-in.

Now let's take another exercise to know how strong your communication strength is, reflect on the following questions relating to communication strengths. And then grade yourself mentally if you're doing well in this aspect or not. However, even if you think you're good in this aspect, that shouldn't stop you from strengthening your skills further. Don't worry as we go along in this section, I will show you ways how to go about strengthening your strengths.

Do you verbalize your outcomes (not tasks) clearly and concisely?
❏ Y ❏ N

If yes, good job. If not, don't worry this can be improved by focusing on the result and getting clarity and agreement on the ideal outcome.

List 5 strategies that you can use to communicate your ideas clearly and concisely with the ideal outcomes in mind and get an agreement on the same.

1._____

_____

2._____

_____

3._____

_____

4._____

_____

5._____

_____

One of the key foundations to optimally effective communication is to know your stuff (your field) better than anyone else out there and be the best expert. The most important trait of you knowing your stuff like the back of your hand is you able to make someone truly feel that you know your stuff without you ever having to mention it.

Are you able to make others feel that you know your stuff better than anyone else without you ever explicitly saying it? ☐ Y ☐ N

If yes, that's good, but you can take it a step further by practicing more that you can even talk about it when under pressure. If not, then this is the first thing you need to do before you think of trying to verbalize your "stuff" to your team and your customers, or anyone else.

Know your stuff, so much so, that when someone wakes you up even from a deep sleep to talk about it, you can do so without blinking. Albert Einstein once said which is "if you can't explain it simply, then you did not understand it well enough"[1]. Also, know your stuff so well that you can explain it using analogies that your audience can relate to.

A salient aspect of effective communication is listening.

Do you genuinely listen when your teammates are talking to you?
❏ Y ❏ N

If yes, that's good, your team will know that their thoughts and concerns are being heard and their productivity will be high as they feel they are part of the bigger picture. If not, you need to understand and acknowledge the emotions of the speaker, confirm what you have heard, and offer the next steps. Not sentence listening, word listening, pretend listening, pretend listening, selective listening, or self-centered listening. Please see an example below:

"I understand you are frustrated. You mentioned or I heard you say .... Am I correct?
Would you like to ......? Or would ......as the next step work for you?"

You can see a massive transformation in your workplace once you incorporate "genuine listening." Let's identify areas in your business where you can instill the same.

What are five situations or areas in the business where you can practice "genuine listening"?

1._____

_____

2._____

_____

3._____

_____

4._____

_____

5._____

_____

The second piece of communication is talking. Some of the important skills that can make you an effective talker are

1. Paraphrasing (summarizing in 5 words or less first, then expanding, and asking if you need to expand any further or if the listener understood)

2. Displaying empathy vs pity (example: I am so sorry vs I understand what you are going through. I once had (a story...) I am so sorry you have to... and then what was done to deal with the situation...)

3. Sharing experiences, stories, and readings

4. Providing Support

5. Providing Feedback instead of criticism and asking for commitment or agreement on the feedback and next steps.

The next step is to incorporate these good habits into your routines. Routines bring freedom from stress. It helps you cope with difficult situations and stressful environments as well.

What are five routines you can incorporate into your business that will allow you to be Sharing, Supportive, Empathetic, To the Point, and a great leader that provides great feedback?

1._____

_____

2._____

_____

3._____

_____

4._____

_____

5._____

_____

Now that you understand breaking the communication bottleneck, the biggest bottleneck that exists in businesses of all sizes, you are ready to embark on the "confidence journey" by using the tool on the next page.

When you use this tool effectively it will help you leverage your strengths to build more confidence in your personal life and your workplace.

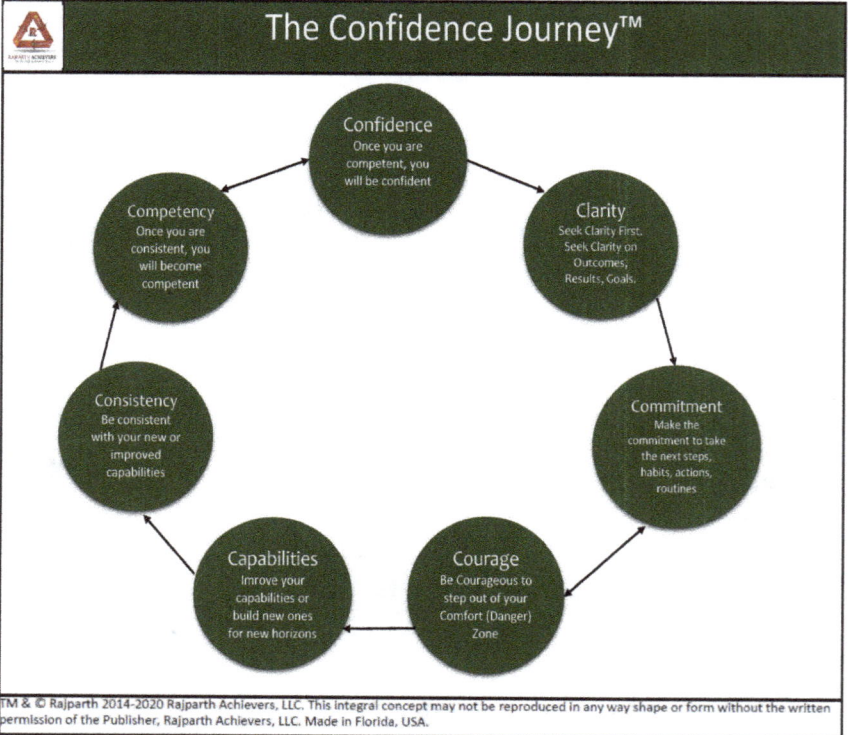

The Confidence Journey™

Confidence — Once you are competent, you will be confident

Clarity — Seek Clarity First. Seek Clarity on Outcomes; Results, Goals.

Commitment — Make the commitment to take the next steps; habits, actions, routines

Courage — Be Courageous to step out of your Comfort (Danger) Zone

Capabilities — Improve your capabilities or build new ones for new horizons

Consistency — Be consistent with your new or improved capabilities

Competency — Once you are consistent, you will become competent

Now, let's build one sample confidence journey so you can replicate the process for any aspect.

1. Clarity- What are the areas in your business and life you need Clarity?

What are the goals or outcomes you are trying to reach in these areas?

Is each of these goals aligned with your 5-year Moonshot and 25-year Vision? ☐ Y ☐ N

If yes, you can move on to the next step of the confidence journey. If not, please get Book #1 to build a clear 5-year Moonshot, a 25-year vision, a 3-year goal, and a One-year plan to achieve your three-year goal in one year. Until the goals are aligned, keep repeating the exercise. The key word here is goals and not desires. Goals are measurable and can be related to an activity or strategy whereas desires are just wishes. There is a very fine line between the two. For example, in a business goal, you could say "I want to make $10 million in revenues"- this is a desire. "I want to make $10 million by selling my $10,000 best-seller service to 1000 ideal Johns (a profile of an ideal customer) in a 10-mile radius in a year" is a goal. "I want to lose 10 pounds" is a desire and not a goal. "I will do 30 minutes of cardio and 30 minutes of strength exercise 3 times a week to lose 10 pounds in 6 months" is a goal.

A goal is something that you're willing to work to achieve, you have complete control over the situation. While a desire is something you wish for, you don't have complete control over how to acquire it.

The next step is to build commitment or build the courage to commit.

A commitment is something you never give up until it is fulfilled. It comes with the responsibility to take it to the finish line. This is the state or quality of being dedicated to a cause. Once you have clarity on your goals and have identified the path that will get you there, the next step is to commit to taking the necessary steps and actions toward achieving your goals.

What is the commitment you need to make to achieve the goals you outlined earlier?

_____
_____
_____
_____
_____

Once you commit you need the courage to take the steps or sometimes you need the courage to commit. They go together. Courage is the ability to do something that frightens one. As an entrepreneur, you may already know what you need to do, to take your business to the next level. And you might be scared because it's new territory for you. Everything you want to happen for you in your life and your business is on the other side of fear, and the courage to go after our goals brings about growth in our lives. This step in the confidence journey is telling you to step out of your comfort zone and go conquer. Courage is also mental and not physical. For example, you may need to be courageous to just have a difficult conversation with your partner or team member.

What fears, obstacles, and difficulties do you need to overcome courageously to fulfill your commitment?

_____
_____
_____
_____
_____

Once you courageously take the step to move forward, you need to develop certain capabilities or utilize or improve some of your capabilities. For example, you may need to consult someone before having a difficult conversation with your partner or team member. You may need to do a role-play and that is developing a capability that you may not have had before. Also, you will develop new capabilities and skills as you try to fulfill your commitments courageously.

What specific new skills, capabilities, and talents do you need, or you will develop because of fulfilling your commitment?

_____
_____
_____
_____
_____
_____
_____

Capability is the power or ability to do something. If your identified goals will require capabilities that you don't have, you will need to improve on your existing capabilities by learning the skills required. Or you can hire someone with the required skill set to get that aspect of the job done. To become a master at the new capability, you will need to do it consistently.

Consistency is the quality of always behaving or performing similarly. Consistency in business means that when you have found something that works well in your business, learn to replicate it. Be consistent with your new and improved capabilities.

What consistency do you need to implement to develop mastery or expertise in the capabilities?

_____
_____
_____
_____
_____
_____
_____

Competency is the ability to do something successfully or efficiently well. Once you have become consistent with your new and improved capabilities, gradually you will gain competency in those areas.

At what stage you would feel competent in the capabilities you outlined earlier? (You would define the ultimate test to measure your competence in the same)

Confidence is being sure in yourself and in your abilities to succeed. And this can only come when you are competent in your capabilities. This is the beginning of the infinite loop of the competent-confidence loop. When you are confident, you are competent and when you are competent, you are confident.

When this happens, the sky is no longer your limit, but your starting point. As the next step from here is unlimited growth. I have attached the confidence journey tool. To help you go on a confidence journey, you can print it out, so you can fill it out and keep it in a place where you can see it all the time. Then be sure to build the takeaways from the chapter.

The Confidence Journey™

Start Date: _____   Prepared For: _____   End Date:

Confidence
What's the confidence I have achieved?
_____
_____
_____

Competent
What results or deliverables would make it competent?
_____
_____
_____

Clarity
What Clarity I Need to Seek?
_____
_____
_____

Consistency
At what stage would be my capabilities considered Consistent?
_____
_____
_____

Commitments
What Commitments I need to Make?
_____
_____
_____

Capabilities
What will be my new capabilities?
_____
_____
_____

Courage
What uncomfortable steps or Courage I need to Develop?
_____
_____
_____

Kudos on completing all the exercises and answering all the questions in week one, where you learned about the strength-confidence loop. In week two, you will the WMDs in your business and how to disarm them. The disarmament will revolutionize your business.

Before you head off to week two, please check out the next page, where you will have the chance to write the takeaways from this chapter that can assist you in leveraging your topmost strengths and working on the biggest one in the next 90 days; this will greatly facilitate in achieving your three-year goal in one year.

P.S.: attached on the next page are useful resources that you should check out, as they will be of immense help to you.

Week 1

Your Chapter Takeaways

What are your top 5 STRENGTHS you want to leverage?

1. _____
   _____
2. _____
   _____
3. _____
   _____
4. _____
   _____
5. _____
   _____

What is that ONE STRENGTH you need to work on in the next 90 Days that will help you get better in 2023?

_____
_____
_____
_____
_____
_____

Useful Resources

QR Code to scan and get all FREE Tools and Resources:

Link from the QR Code:

https://linktr.ee/TheOneYearBreakthrough

Link to all my events:

https://www.eventbrite.com/o/bimal-shah-7943115300

Time to Celebrate

Before you move to the next chapter, take time to celebrate.

Here are five little ways you can celebrate:

1. Watch a movie at the IMAX theatre- it is a great experience.
2. Go running in your community with your pet if you can.
3. Go out to dine at a restaurant cuisine that you have never done before- maybe Peruvian cuisine.
4. Go for a long drive by the oceanside with your other half and drive with your windows down to enjoy the wind.
5. Go shopping for yourself and buy something nice that you always wanted and is more than an amount that you normally don't spend instantly or randomly.

Week 2

The WMD System

When you read the title, it is not Weapons of Mass destruction or distraction but a "Weakness Management and Discharge" system. I used to think that you should hide your weaknesses, so no one knows about them. Now I know there is a way to discharge them—like you get a discharge when you get out from a hospital or a doctor's office because you are fine and all the things that needed to be done are done. Let me share a story.

Nobody is perfect and everyone has some weaknesses or the other. I had many. I can talk about my first speaking engagement which was in a restaurant with 18 people and using the slide projector where you must manually put each transparency in front of the glass. Whatever you could think of go wrong did go wrong from the food, the bulb going out, transparency slides getting jumbled and falling on the floor, and the wrong information on the slides-Yet I took a breather and connected with the audience in front of me and just started talking and asking questions. In the end, I had 6 clients from the audience!

That's a hell of a WMD system- don't you think?

Below I would walk you through a series of mindset exercises, tools, and the next steps in building the WMD. Many a time, we call our inabilities weaknesses because we are unable to be effective or do things right. It is just your inability to get it done right and there is a process to get it done right.

The W- The Weakness Discovery

In this stage, you will go through a series of questions to understand your true weaknesses. We often have a misconception about our weaknesses. I did too. I had a misunderstanding that my weakness was in the delegation of tasks. I used to do it myself instead of delegating it and then I realized my true weakness was in the verbalization of what needed to be achieved. I was so good at writing it out rather than verbalizing it. So now, I delegate so much with complete clarity on the outcomes and boundaries. I followed the same steps below which helped me do the same.

What do you consider your biggest inabilities that hinder your progress in life?

_____

_____

_____

_____

_____

_____

What do you consider your biggest inabilities that hinder your progress in business?

_____

_____

_____

_____

_____

_____

One of the ways to easily manage the weaknesses is WHO and not HOW.

Who would be able to help you manage your weaknesses in life?

_____

Who would be able to help you manage your weaknesses in business?

_____

Are there weaknesses that you need to find a way to manage yourself?
❑ Y ❑ N

If yes, you can move on to the next steps. If not, that's great-- all you need is a list of WHOs. You have already done more than half of the work, now all that remains is to learn how to manage your weaknesses. I will walk you through it.

Please perform the following exercises even if you think you have all your weaknesses figured out. It might surprise you to know that some of your weaknesses may have escaped you. Now we move to the "M" stage of the WMD system.

The M- The Management of Weaknesses

Think of activities or tasks that you are incompetent and whenever you try doing them, you fail at them consistently.

What are the top 5 activities that you feel you are incompetent at?

1. _____
   _____
2. _____
   _____
3. _____
   _____
4. _____
   _____
5. _____

The next step is to find a way to manage your weaknesses. You need to break down each of your weaknesses into small elements and understand where in each of the weaknesses you are truly weak. For example, you may consider delegation of tasks as your weakness but there may be several elements- maybe you are afraid to delegate because you feel they won't get it right or maybe you feel you have an inability or don't have the patience to explain how to do the task or maybe it is something else. Once you understand, you will find a way to manage the weakness. For example, if you discover it is your patience to explain how the task is supposed to be done, then you can focus on communicating the outcome you want as you are very clear on what outcome you want and let your team member figure out how it needs to be done.

Please take one of the weaknesses you listed above and break it into minor components.

_____
_____
_____
_____
_____
_____
_____
_____

What clarity did you receive from the above answer?

_____
_____
_____

What is the action you need to take to manage your above-mentioned weakness?

_____
_____
_____
_____

Another way to manage your weaknesses is to talk to trusted and successful people you know who have overcome the weakness you identified and see what they did and what advice they have for you.

Who are the top five people you will contact to discuss your top five weaknesses?

1. _____
   _____

2. _____
   _____

3. _____
   _____

4. _____
   _____

5. _____
   _____

Congratulations on completing the above exercise. Because writing down how to manage your weakness is the most effective way to start managing them. Now we move to the "D" stage of the WMD system. This is the discharge of the weaknesses.

The D- The Discharge of Weaknesses

The discharge happens when you can let go, or the weaknesses find a way to exit from your mind or your body, or your system.

The fundamental element that keeps your weaknesses weak is your Fears. The real fear is your inability or knowledge or skill not knowing what needs to be done in the event of a situation. You feel "Frozen" many a time. So, to unfreeze yourself, you need to face your fears. It is like putting water on the ice until it melts and then cleaning it up. By facing your fears, you control the fears instead of having them control you. The most non-threatening way to face your fear is to write them down. The paper or the notepad or book where you write isn't going to do anything to you or say anything to you. If anything, it will provide great insights. We all have certain fears and saying to yourself that you don't fear anything is a lie. So be honest with yourself as it is just you and this book.

What are the top five things you are afraid of, that is/may be holding you back from achieving your goals or the intended outcomes or making you weak in what you identified earlier?

1._____

_____

2._____

_____

3._____

_____

4._____

_____

5._____

_____

Now that we have those written down, we can work towards facing them. The goal here is to discharge these fears by "unfreezing" these fears. Unfreezing can happen physically or psychologically. An example of a physical barrier could be: "I have Plantar Fasciitis and my fear is I can't travel anywhere there is a lot of walking." The way you could unfreeze that physical barrier is to write "I will go to physical therapy once a week and get special shoes that allow me to walk comfortably without causing any further pain." Similarly, an example of a psychological barrier could be "I fear talking about terminating my employee and I will just send an official letter instead."

What are the physical barriers you need to overcome to unfreeze your fears? (If none, you can skip and move to the next one).

_____

_____

_____

_____

_____

_____

What are the psychological barriers you need to overcome to unfreeze your fears?

_____

_____

_____

_____

_____

_____

What are the top five strategies that would deliver the highest payoff and overcome the barriers most optimally and effectively that are sustainable and will create a permanent discharge of the weaknesses that you identified?

1._____

_____

2._____

_____

3._____

_____

4._____

_____

5._____

_____

Who needs to do what by when to fully execute the strategies you identified earlier and take it to a finish line?

1._____

_____

2._____

_____

3._____

_____

4._____

_____

5._____

_____

Many a time Fears are false myths in our mind that appear very real because all the logic points us towards the same. I realized this when my wife told me that her fears are not fears and are just her way of cautioning on what could go wrong. This is when I started replacing my mental or psychological fears and hers with the word "caution" and identifying if it is red or yellow. Red means turning back, and yellow meaning proceeding with caution.

Fears are not bad at all if you consider them as caution signs and not as panic signs- never make any decisions out of panic and out of fear- Rather strive to always become a leader and your highest self and ask what your highest self will do in the situation. One of the most common mistakes or decisions that are made in business is shortchanging your self-worth because you need the money. You must have heard the saying "beggars can't be choosers." That is not true- if you portray your self-worth properly and deliver value ethically, you will get the money you rightfully can.

One of the most common fears you need to discharge for business is panic or "victim" based decision-making. We make our minds go to that victim-based mentality so quickly and so easily in life and business that it is unbelievable. The next steps will help you discharge that victim-based mindset.

What are the top 10 decisions you tend to make or have made in the past with a "victim-based" mindset?

1._____

_____

2._____

_____

3._____

_____

4._____

_____

5._____

_____

6._____

_____

7._____
_____
8._____
_____
9._____
_____
0._____
_____

If you were the highest self that you can attain as a status and you were
a strong leader in those same situations, what would be the alternate
decisions you would have made in those ten circumstances?

1._____
_____
2._____
_____
3._____
_____
4._____
_____
5._____
_____
6._____
_____
7._____
_____
8._____
_____
9._____
_____
10._____
_____

Do you see the difference in your decisions? The next step to get a complete discharge from the most common weakness experienced in business is to act.

Who needs to do what by when to prevent yourself from taking "victim-mindset" decisions in the future in the circumstances outlined above and all other situations?

This will allow you to have a proper discharge. On the next page, I have outlined how to use The WMD System frequently.

The WMD System

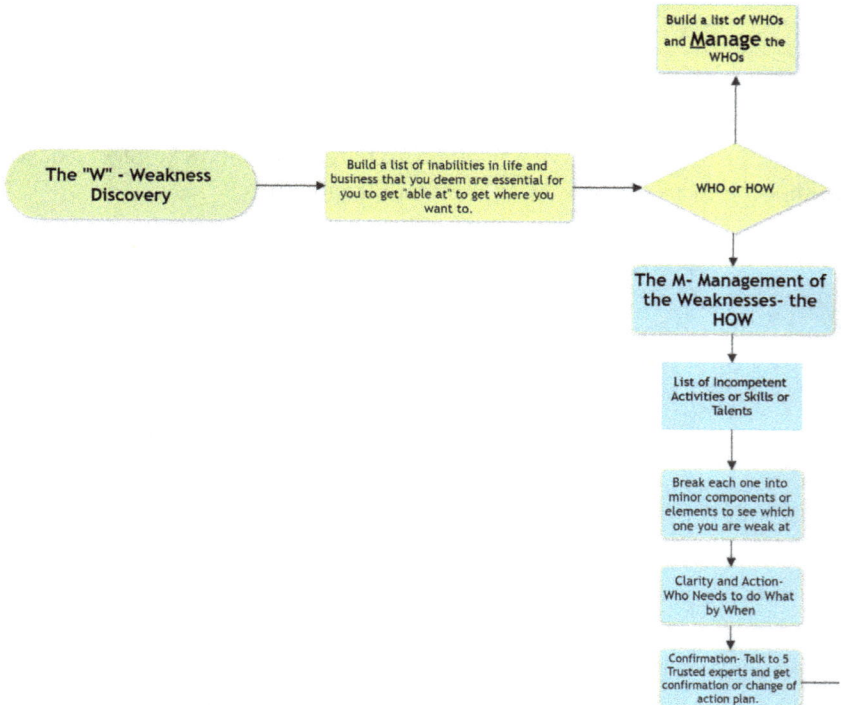

```
The "W" - Weakness          Build a list of inabilities in life and        WHO or HOW
Discovery                   business that you deem are essential for
                            you to get "able at" to get where you
                            want to.
```

Build a list of WHOs
and **Manage** the
WHOs

The M- Management of
the Weaknesses- the
HOW

List of Incompetent
Activities or Skills or
Talents

Break each one into
minor components or
elements to see which
one you are weak at

Clarity and Action-
Who Needs to do What
by When

Confirmation- Talk to 5
Trusted experts and get
confirmation or change of
action plan.

The WMD System

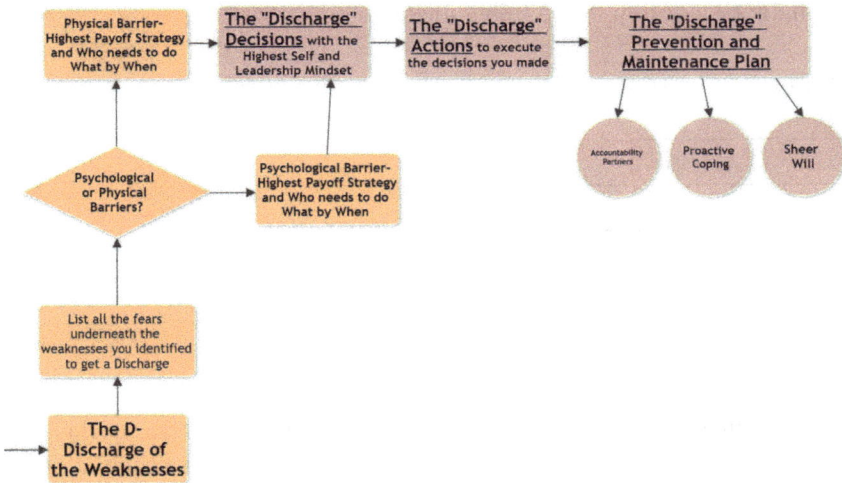

```
Physical Barrier-          The "Discharge"        The "Discharge"          The "Discharge"
Highest Payoff Strategy    Decisions with the     Actions to execute       Prevention and
and Who needs to do        Highest Self and       the decisions you made   Maintenance Plan
What by When               Leadership Mindset
```

Physical Barrier-Highest Payoff Strategy and Who needs to do What by When

The "Discharge" Decisions with the Highest Self and Leadership Mindset

The "Discharge" Actions to execute the decisions you made

The "Discharge" Prevention and Maintenance Plan

Accountability Partners

Proactive Coping

Sheer Will

Psychological or Physical Barriers?

Psychological Barrier-Highest Payoff Strategy and Who needs to do What by When

List all the fears underneath the weaknesses you identified to get a Discharge

The D-Discharge of the Weaknesses

The WMD System Prevention and Maintenance Plan

Just like when you get out of a hospital or an urgent care center or a doctor's office, they will give you a prevention and maintenance plan, you need a preventive and maintenance plan to make sure your weaknesses don't surface again.

There are three main methods of the prevention plan, and you can choose all three or one or a combination. There are more methods, but these three have proven to work.

1. *Accountability Partners:*

You need to have an accountability partner who holds you accountable for your actions and decisions and that you have regularly scheduled accountability meetings or conversations. Do these enough times until it is a habit or a system that is fully functional on its own.

Who would be your ideal accountability buddy and why?

_____

_____

_____

_____

_____

_____

An accountability buddy to you as an entrepreneur should be another entrepreneur whom you agree to stay in touch with and give reports on your progress in overcoming your weakness, and he or she will do the same with you.

Accountability buddies are more than friends, they motivate you to get things done and hold you to your work commitment. They don't hesitate to tell you the truth and tell you things that you may not want to hear or may not make you feel good.

Please note that your accountability buddy is not your boss, and you're not superior to them either. You both are equal. You check in on each other regularly. And the simple pressure of having to report to someone is enough to help us break out of our weaknesses. As it's embarrassing to tell someone "I didn't do what I said would do"

2. *Proactive Coping:*

Proactive coping is a positive coping strategy, whereby one reduces the stress of a difficult challenge by anticipating what it will be like and preparing for how one is going to cope with it. You can cope with difficult challenges by learning the skill you lack. The most effective tool I have created to do proactive coping is The Implementation Guarantor™ where you can put all the review dates as the actual deadlines on the calendar and proactively understand the obstacles or the barriers you face. Once you understand the barriers or obstacles, you will build the highest payoff strategies. If you aren't sure what the highest payoff strategy would be, talk to an expert or research. You will be positively amazed at what you discover.

What would be your strategy for Proactive Coping?

_____

_____

_____

_____

_____

_____

3. *Sheer Will and Commitment:*

There is no question that where there is a will there is a way. There is also a method to conquer your weakness through sheer will and commitment. Maybe you're fed up with a weakness, that's holding you back from taking your business to the next level. You have tried several strategies and they were not successful. And now you are wondering if there's a way to conquer that weakness. Yes, there is, but it's going to take commitment and will.

There are three effective steps to conquer your weakness.

Step 1: *Admit Your Weaknesses with a period*: Admit your weaknesses to your better half who may empathize with you or maybe be sarcastic or laugh at you. That is perfectly fine. The reaction is not important- the admittance is. Admit your weakness. There are no excuses here.

It's not "I am lousy at communicating because I am too busy to do it effectively.' It's "I am lousy at communicating. Period."

Step 2: *Love the weakness*. This step is taking a cue from Toyota's management school, when they find a weakness in production, they are excited by the prospects of improving on their weaknesses. You should learn to do the same. Be excited and thrilled to discover your weakness.

Step 4: *Dashboard it*: Create a dashboard or whiteboard or calendar where you track the progress of your successfully overcoming and managing your weaknesses. Have a target number you want to reach- like want to do this successfully 21 times in a month or a week or 90 days. You need to make conscious efforts to keep track of your progress.

Now if you are still getting stuck, the main element is the why behind the weakness. Why do you want to conquer the weakness? I want you to write down your weaknesses and why you want to break them, knowing your why will help you to achieve your desired goal.

Weakness:

_____

_____

_____

_____

_____

Why you want to conquer it:

_____

_____

_____

_____

_____

Weakness:

_____
_____
_____
_____
_____

Why you want to conquer it:

_____
_____
_____
_____
_____

Weakness:

_____
_____
_____
_____
_____

Why you want to conquer it:

_____
_____
_____
_____
_____

Weakness:

_____
_____
_____
_____
_____

Why you want to conquer it:

_____
_____
_____
_____
_____

Weakness:

_____

_____

_____

_____

_____

Why you want to conquer it:

_____

_____

_____

_____

_____

Congratulations on completing all the exercises and answering all the questions in week two, where you built an amazing WMD System. In week two, you will build The Lever and The Fulcrum which will allow you to move your world and shake things up in a big way.

Before you head off to week three, please check out the next page, where you will have the chance to write your customized WMD system that will allow you to charge forward toward your goals like a bull!!

Please don't forget to check out the FREE tools and Resources page that is like magic because every time you check it there may be additions or something new as I consistently update it.

Week 2

Your Chapter Takeaways

Your "WMD" System

Your W: Your top 5 identified microelements - your True Weaknesses:

1._____

2. _____

3. _____

4. _____

5. _____

Your M: Your "How" or "Who" Management System:

_____
_____
_____
_____
_____
_____

Your D: Your "Discharge" System:

_____
_____
_____
_____
_____
_____
_____
_____

Useful Resources

QR Code to scan and get all FREE Tools and Resources:

Link from the QR Code:

https://linktr.ee/TheOneYearBreakthrough

Link to all my events:

https://www.eventbrite.com/o/bimal-shah-7943115300

Time to Celebrate

Before you move to the next chapter, take time to celebrate.

Here are five little ways you can celebrate:

1. Buy tickets for an Improv or a comedy show for you and your better half.
2. Do tie-dye with one of your plain white t-shirts.
3. Take a painting project for one of your walls.
4. Surprise your family with a nice big wall family picture frame that is also funny and showcases one of your travels.
5. Do a nice car wash for your car by yourself.

Week 3

The Lever and the Fulcrum

Archimedes said, "Give me a lever long enough and a fulcrum to place it on and I shall move the world."[2] You need to have a lever and a fulcrum to move and shake your world. Please see the image below to get an idea...

I used to think you can just start building your business with a lever and I was wrong. Now I know that building a strong and long lever and a fulcrum in a business has an everlasting impact.

Let me share how I built the lever and the fulcrum for myself and my business. Every time, I work with a client I tell them I will come into the kitchen and cook with them. So, my process was "doing it with you" rather than telling you what to do. This 13-book series is also written with a "doing with you" premise as at the end of the day, this book series becomes the book series that you would cherish forever as you have written your dreams, actions, decisions, plans, and much more in it. The strong and long lever was the 100-plus thinking tools I have built that allow business owners to scale rapidly with ease. The fulcrum is the medium of distribution of how I distribute the concepts and the system, and the book series is one of them. The online university, the software platform, and the Pioneers Academy are other Fulcrums that I use to move other worlds.

Below I would walk you through a series of questions, exercises, thinking tools, and the next steps to help you build your lever and fulcrum for your business. The first step in building your lever and fulcrum is to identify the world that you want to move and shake. It could be the biggest barriers and obstacles you want to move. It could be the competition you want to crush. It could be the biggest market share of your ideal customers you want to capture, or it could be making your existing customer base buy all your other products and services. It could be anything you want to move and shake and either get it out of your way or take it to the next level.

What is the world that you want to move and shake?

_____

_____

_____

_____

_____

_____

_____

_____

_____

_____

Now, we will use everything you have learned in the previous two weeks to identify the biggest strengths and weaknesses in your business. First, you will use your identified biggest strengths to overcome 10 of your competitor's biggest weaknesses.

What are the top 10 strengths that your business has over your competitors?

1._____
_____

2._____
_____

3._____
_____

4._____
_____

5._____
_____

6._____
_____

7._____
_____

8._____
_____

9._____
_____

10._____
_____

To help you with this, think of the several advantages your business has over your competitors in terms of the components of your business such as marketing, operations, sales, training and development, innovation, human relations, technology, customer advocacy, finances, and leadership of the company. These advantages are the strengths of your business. Now you want these advantages to strengthen your ability to gain an edge and manage your weaknesses as well. So, it is essential to identify your weaknesses as well. You must be true to yourself and acknowledge your weaknesses. You can look at each of the areas mentioned in this paragraph and see if you have weaknesses in any of those areas.

What are the top 10 weaknesses of your business?

1._____

_____

2._____

_____

3._____

_____

4._____

_____

5._____

_____

6._____

_____

7._____

_____

8._____

_____

9._____

_____

10._____

_____

Now that we have identified the strengths and weaknesses of your business, it is time to identify your best or nearest competitor's strengths and weaknesses. Again, you want to be true to yourself and acknowledge that you have competition and compare their strengths and weaknesses against yours. If you cannot identify weaknesses in your competitors, that means you don't know your competitors well and you need to get to know them very well through research of all methods. It could also mean you pay a visit to your competitor acting as a customer.

What are your competitor's top 10 biggest weaknesses?

1._____

2._____

3._____

4._____

5._____

6._____

7._____

8._____

9._____

10._____

Now think of ways that you can use your 10 biggest strengths to overcome 10 of your competitor's biggest weaknesses.

_____
_____
_____
_____
_____
_____
_____
_____
_____
_____
_____
_____
_____

It could be that your customer retention rate is high, and that of your competitors is low when compared to yours. You will need to think of ways to ensure that your customers are loyal to your brand, and don't even give a second thought about your competitors. You do this by making your customers feel special. Whatever you use, that is helping you build a long and strong lever. Again, if you can't come up with the strengths of your nearest and best competitors -you don't know them well enough and you need to research to get to know them very well.

What are your competitor's 10 biggest strengths?

1._____
_____

2._____
_____

3._____
_____

4._____
_____

5._____
_____

6._____
_____

7._____
_____

8._____
_____

9._____
_____

10._____
_____

Now you need to look at the meaningful transformations in your business. How can you transform your business weaknesses, to make them at par or better than your competitor's strengths?

For example, if your competitor has more branding and marketing present than you, then you must think of what is it that you need to start doing to improve your marketing and branding. It could be that you need to invest in advertising, or you need to be strategic in your advertising. So, the right people can rightly know about your great products and how they have an edge over everyone else. Thereby giving your customers a run for their money.

The above strategies that I have shared with you work. I have used them to transform the lives of companies. For example, there was a construction company that hired me to help them polish their proposals so they could beat the competition.

What I did was to help the company identify and include 5 of its biggest strengths in their company and helped build its Lever. And guess what, these strengths cost the customer $0.00.

I just made the following updates to their proposal.

Showing up on time for the job:	Cost $0.00
Doing the job on time:	Cost $0.00
Minimal change orders:	Cost $0.00
Following strict safety protocols on the job:	Cost $0.00
Fair and ethical pricing with strict compliance:	Cost $0.00
No surprises in Parts:	Cost $0.00

These were the first line items they put on their proposals, and they won twice the number of bids and crushed their competition!

The fulcrum for this lever was to put these on their proposals for their bids!!

If you have difficulty or need assistance building your lever and fulcrum, please click or visit https://bit.ly/callbimal

To go deeper and help you identify the weaknesses of your competition, you can go into each function of the business and build your competitor's weaknesses and see how you can make them your strengths.

I have shown an illustration on the next page on how focusing on each function of the business helps you build a strong and long lever that allows you to place it on a fulcrum of your choice to move the biggest barriers and obstacles in your business or shake your world or move it to the next level.

You can complete all the questions that follow the illustration to build the strongest lever and the right fulcrum to place it on.

Let's start with each of those functions and they are in no specific order or priority. You can decide the order and priority based on the nature of your business.

Your Biggest Obstacles and Barriers to Your Next level Growth or Taking your World to the next level or your business to the next level or even your customers to the next level

Customer Advocacy

Finances

HR

Sales

Operations

Technology

Innovation

Leadership

Training

Marketing

Your Platform - Your Medium

What are the weaknesses of your competition in marketing?

_____
_____
_____
_____
_____

For example, the weakness of your competition in marketing can be that they do traditional marketing only, they don't do online marketing, and they lack a social media presence.

How can you make the weakness of your competition in marketing your strength?

_____
_____
_____
_____

For example, you have identified that your competition lacks an online presence, you can make this your strength by establishing a solid brand presence with targeted marketing, with the right content marketing strategy to sell your company, thereby dominating the ideal target online.

What are the weaknesses of your competition in operations?

_____
_____
_____
_____
_____
_____

For example, your competition might be experiencing weaknesses in logistics, or operational excellence, and/or providing a dream-come-true experience to the customer every time. You can build a dream-come-true experience for your customer with operational excellence and knock out your competition.

How can you make the weakness of your competition in operations your strength?

_____
_____
_____
_____
_____
_____
_____
_____

After you have built the dream-come-true experience for your customer and it works like clockwork, you can use that to create more sales.

What are the weaknesses of your competition in sales?

_____
_____
_____
_____

Many a time the sales team is doing a poor job on sales, or the competition may not have a sales team. You can get an edge with a lean optimal sales team and some "guarantees."- For example "guaranteed response within 4 hours" or "Guaranteed same-day service". I offer a 500% ROI or 5X ROI Guarantee on anyone who works with me and hires for our consulting or coaching. Guarantees help you get Sales.

How can you make the weakness of your competition in sales your strength?

_____

_____

_____

_____

_____

Training and development are key to any organization. Complete and comprehensive training brings productive output and profitability to your business. If you get an edge over your competition on training and development, you could be far ahead in the results with your customers.

What are the weaknesses of your competition in training and development?

_____

_____

_____

_____

_____

_____

How can you make the weakness of your competition in training and development your strength?

_____

_____

_____

_____

An additional essential function in business is innovation. You can get an edge over your competitors is the ability to quickly bring in innovation. The faster you can innovate, the faster you can outsmart or kill your competition.

What are the weaknesses of your competition in innovation?

_____

_____

_____

_____

How can you make the weakness of your competition in innovation your strengths?

_____

_____

_____

_____

_____

If there is a four-letter word for business success, it is "HIRE." You need to get your hiring right and hire the right people. If you have long-term stable employees, it can be easily highlighted in your advertising and marketing to help you get an edge over your competitors. It also attracts good talent.

What are the weaknesses of your competition in HR (I call it Human Relations instead of Human Resources)?

_____

_____

_____

_____

How can you make the weakness of your competition in HR your strengths?

_____

_____

_____

_____

_____

Technology is an absolute necessity in any business and a business with advanced technology and platforms can have a substantial edge over its competition and many a time be more affordable than the competition.

What are the weaknesses of your competition in technology?

_____
_____
_____
_____

How can you make the weakness of your competition in technology your strengths?

_____
_____
_____
_____

Leadership can play a key role in crushing the competition or building a strategic direction that paves the way for continued sustainability and success. You can get a substantial edge with great leadership or upper management team in your company.

What are the weaknesses of your competition in leadership and management?

_____
_____
_____
_____

How can you make the weakness of your competition in technology your strengths?

_____
_____
_____
_____

Next is customer advocacy. Customer Advocacy is much bigger than customer service. Customer Advocacy means your team and your people are advocates of the customers and listen to everything the customer has to say, do the right thing, or meet with the right team members or management to get a win-win for both the customer and the company. This would make raving fans in your company rather than just customers.

What are the weaknesses of your competition in customer advocacy?

_____
_____
_____
_____

How can you make the weakness of your competition in customer advocacy your strength?

_____
_____
_____
_____

The financial situation of your business, the profitability, and the balance sheet are very important. Maybe your competitors lack financial muscle, and you do, and you can use that as leverage to excel. It could be that you have a very quality customer base and a healthy profitable cash flow compared to your competition and that can help you build long-term sustainability instead of short-term gains. Use it.

What are the weaknesses of your competition in finance?

_____
_____
_____
_____
_____
_____
_____

How can you make the weaknesses of your competition in finance your strengths?

_____
_____
_____
_____

R&D happens in every business. It may take a different form or category, but it does exist. You can discover the weaknesses of Research & Development in your competitors and see how you excel compared to them.

What are the weaknesses of your competition in R&D?

_____

_____

_____

_____

_____

_____

_____

How can you make the weaknesses of your competition in R&D your strengths?

_____

_____

_____

_____

By looking at each essential function in your business, you have built a very strong lever and the ability to place it on an ideal fulcrum of your choice. You may have additional functions in your business that may not be covered here, but you can use the same system for any function. You will move your world with the lever and fulcrum you build.

Kudos on completing week three, where you learned how to build the lever and fulcrum of your business. You may be wondering where you are going to find the time to execute all of this. That's precisely what I address in the next chapter. You will discover the hidden secrets of how to make freedom of time. You will discover that time is just a construct in your mind and if you change the construct, you free up time. Are you curious about this? See you in week four. Do check out the free resources provided for your good on the next page, before heading off to week 4.

Congratulations on building or improving the strengths in each function of the business and building your Lever, building your Fulcrum, and identifying the world you want to move and shake. It will continue to take you a long way. In week four, you will build The Freedom of Time which allows you to build and chase infinite possibilities.

Before you head off to week three, please check out the next page, where you will have the chance to summarize your customized lever and fulcrum and shake and move your world as Archimedes said!!

Please don't forget to check out the FREE tools and Resources page that is like magic because every time you check it there may be additions or something new as I consistently update it.

Week 3

Your Chapter Takeaways

Describe the World that you want to move and shake.

_____
_____
_____
_____
_____
_____
_____
_____
_____

Describe your strongest and longest lever:

_____
_____
_____
_____
_____
_____
_____

Describe the ideal fulcrum that you want to place it on:

_____
_____
_____
_____
_____
_____
_____

Useful Resources

QR Code to scan and get all FREE Tools and Resources:

Link from the QR Code:

https://linktr.ee/TheOneYearBreakthrough

Link to all my events:

https://www.eventbrite.com/o/bimal-shah-7943115300

Time to Celebrate

Before you move to the next chapter, take time to celebrate.

Here are five little ways you can celebrate:

1. Connect with the most important world of yours- your family – Play Code Names- it can go on for hours.
2. Take a lesson on drawing from YouTube – there are many channels that teach you amazing drawings for free.
3. Paint one of your walls with Dry-erase pain that could become your vision wall.
4. Make a cocktail drink that is very difficult to make. Go and buy all the ingredients that are needed. I am sure there is a YouTube video on how to make it.
5. Buy something nice for your favorite car.

Week 4

Making Freedom of Time

I used to think that working all the time is the way to grow the business. Now I know that being disconnected makes you exponentially productive. Have you ever wondered what is the one thing entrepreneurs gravitate the most to in business? It is "Freedom" So this week I am going to talk about how to free up 15 hours or more every week for yourself and your family. But before that, I would like to share a story of how the exercise of looking to free up time added multi-millions in revenues and the right business decisions.

This is the story of a CEO of a 12-employee company whose time was eaten up by the day-to-day minutia. We used my Business Scorecard tool (You can get all the details and the tool in Book No. 3) on her and realized that freeing up 15 hours or more allowed her to meet at least three CEOs and that translated into $3.5 million in sales. For the day-to-day minutia, through our unique hiring system, she was able to hire one individual who was the best hire in 30 years in the business and was a CTO, CFO, and COO in one. When we started looking, she and everyone in the company thought I was crazy, and that it was impossible. When it became a reality, even her best entrepreneur friend was shocked and happy.

Now that you know the impossible is possible, Below I would walk you through a series of questions, exercises, thinking tools, and next steps to help you free up 15 or more hours of your week so you can make happen the impossible and scale to the next level.

As mentioned earlier, time is a construct- a theory in your mind. If you change that theory, you change the system, and you change the output. Let's work on that construct.

Do you believe that time can be managed? ☐ Y ☐ N
If yes, why do you believe so?

_____
_____
_____
_____

If not, why do you believe so?

_____
_____
_____
_____
_____
_____

Time can't be managed. Manage means "control or change the direction of ....". You cannot "control or change the direction of time itself." What you do within your time can be managed. What can be managed are the priorities within a set time. Also, time lost can never be regained. Therefore, you always need a system for priority management.

Do you have a to-do list? ☐ Y ☐ N

If yes, do you find it effective? Does it give you stress? Do you feel that it is ever-growing and never-ending? Do you get overwhelmed by it? Do you feel some things never get done from it? If you answered Yes to all or some of these questions, please describe how you feel about the to-do list and what would you like to do about it. If you answered no to some or all of the above, please move to the next question.

If not, what do you use to plan your activities for the day?

Most people think having a to-do list helps them manage their priorities. But this is wrong because a lot of people end up not ticking any tasks as done on the to-do list. As they dread some tasks saying it drains their energy or they feel some tasks are not urgent, so they procrastinate.

I don't have any to-do lists. You may be surprised- right? I have a different approach. I build what I call a "Victories to choose from" list. This way my mind is always looking at prioritizing and not just doing everything.

So you might ask, instead of using a To-Do list, what do I use then? I have a "Victories List" that I prioritize and work on one big victory after another. If the victories list doesn't work for you, you can use the system below that works for anyone who uses it. It is the three-bucket list.

The three buckets are a To-Do now list, a To-Do Later (with date), and a Not-to-do list.

A "To-Do Now" list is a list of outcomes that you have to achieve "now". You must define what "now" means to you. It could be the same day, 24 hours, or 48 hours. I wouldn't define now beyond 48 hours. Anything beyond 48 hours can fall into the "To-Do Later" bucket and you have to assign a timeline to each outcome- three days, one week, 15 days, one month, 45 days, 90 days, and one year. I wouldn't have a timeline beyond one year. For example one of the items that could go in a "one-year timeline" could be a month-long vacation to a favorite place.

What does your To Do now list consists of?

The next stage is to calendar all these outcomes (as you can see I never call anything a task, I say outcomes- outcomes allow you to focus on the result and not the task itself). The calendar is your most powerful "priority management" system and unfortunately, most people don't use it for that as they use the calendar for just regular meetings that they have and not for things that they want to achieve throughout the day.

Is there enough time in your Calendar in the next two days to accomplish all the "To-Do Now" outcomes? ❏ Y ❏ N

If yes, that is great. Maybe you have additional time left to achieve additional outcomes as well. Maybe you have an insight that if you have all this time why you couldn't do the same previously? One reason could be "surfing." Yes- surfing. You surf through social media, you surf through the internet, you surf through the news, you surf through the TV, you surf through your email, you surf through the text messages or messages on social media, you surf through while having a coffee in your hand and gossiping your way to your desk, you surf through your junk mail, you surf through many things in life including the dashboard on your car....

Yes, surfing can take up a lot of your time without you knowing it. Now let's move to your "To-Do Later List." This list must be carefully prepared as the deadlines you give to each project or outcome can impact positively or negatively achieving your three-year goal in one year or doubling your business in a year.

The optimally effective way to look at preparing your "To-Do Later" list on the next pages is to look at the impact it will have short-term and long-term on each and then pencil in the timeline for each. The most essential additional tool you would need to use is "The Implementation Guarantor™" which was provided earlier. When the two are used in conjunction, magic happens. You see a clear possibility for each of the outcomes, you become a great delegator, and you learn how to eliminate, optimize, automate, and delegate.

This list contains important outcomes, but they don't have to be done immediately. But it is these outcomes that take you to the next level. So, working on your "To-Do Later" list is very essential, and more essential is to see how many of those outcomes you can move to "To-Do Now" and how many of the outcomes from the "To-Do Now" aren't essential at all. Focus on eliminating first rather than doing. When you eliminate, you free up time. You see things differently; you do things differently and it brings excitement!!

The To-Do Later List™

Prepared For_____

Start Date:_____ Biggest Achievement:_____ End Date:_____

Results that you want to Achieve	What is the Short Term Impact of this outcome?	Aligned with 3-Year Goal - Y/N	What is the long-term impact of this ouctome?	Aligned with your 3-year Goal- Y/N	What strategy will you implement to get both in alignment?

The To-Do Later List™

Prepared For_____

Start Date:_____ Biggest Achievement:_____ End Date:_____

3 Days (Check Mark)	7 Days (Check Mark)	15 Days (Check Mark)	30 Days (Check Mark)	45 Days (Check Mark)	90 Days (Check Mark)

Once you have completed the "To-Do Later List", it is now time to move on to the "Not-to-Do List." This is the most essential list as this list is one that will help you identify all the habits, routines, and things that you don't need to do that take up a lot of your time.

This is a list that also contains your impulsive decisions that you're tempted to engage in, and they don't bring much improvement to you or your work, instead of doing meaningful tasks. For example, chatting on your phone or watching a movie. I encountered one business owner who had political news and notifications enabled on his phone and he was getting that every 30 seconds and he was in the restaurant business!! There was no connection and there were so many issues happening in his restaurant as he was distracted twice every minute! Once that was eliminated, there was so much productivity in his restaurant.

The Not-to-Do list consists of many elements, and I put the short list below to help you build it using the tool on the next page

Elements to think about to include in your NOT-TO-DO LIST				
Habits	Greed	Victim Mindset	Forgetfulness	Envy
Routines	Addiction (Ex: Surfing)	Fixed Mindset	Saying Yes	Worriedness
Decisions	Anger	Complain and Get Mindset	Multi-Tasking (You only do Background Tasking or Switch Tasking)	Going in too many directions
Activities	Ego	Procrastinate	No Investing (You must invest to get an ROI)	Hating or not enjoying what you do daily.

I am attaching a tool for the Not-to-do list builder. It will guide you in building your Not-to-do list, I will also attach a sample of how I used it for myself, so you can further draw insights on how to use it.

The Not-to-Do List Builder™

Name: _____
Start Date: _____   End Date: _____
Project: _____

What are the top 5 impulsive decisions that haven't brought much improvement in you or your work?	What were the reasons or circumstances that caused that decision to be made?	If you had to make that decision all over again, what are the things you will not do or repeat again?	What are the top 5 logical decisions that haven't brought much improvement in you or your work?	If you had to make the decisions all over again, what are things you will not do repeat again?

What are the top habits, disciplines, or strategies you need to develop or change to accommodate the not-to-do list items?				
1		4	7	10
2		5	8	11
3		6	9	12

Who needs to do what by when to get the not-to-do list in action				

The Not-to-Do List Builder™

Name: Bimal Shah
Start Date: 06/08/2015 End Date: 06/08/2015
Project: My Not-to-do-List

What are the top 5 impulsive decisions that haven't brought much improvement in you or your work?	What were the reasons or circumstances that caused that decision to be made?	If you had to make that decision all over again, what are the things you will not do or repeat again?	What are the top 5 logical decisions that haven't brought much improvement in you or your work?	If you had to make the decisions all over again, what are things you will not do or repeat again?
Spending on latest tech	A belief I need to be up-to-date in technology	Only have tech that can make things faster, easier, cheaper	Spending a lot on Seminars	Only workshops
Buying Movie DVDs in Bulk	To watch movies late night	No late-night movies	Ineffective advertising	Direct-response only
Eating unhealthy Food	Everybody else is eating it	Eat healthy foods only, exercise	Non-fee Customers	Fee Customers
Using too many credit cards	Thinking Credit as Money	Use only one card	Working late	Sleep Early
Last Minute Travel bookings	Belief seminars are good	Travel plans booked in advance	Taking on too much	Delegate

The Not-to-do-List. Start with words I will not......	1- I will not stay awake beyond 10:30	4 I will not drink soda	7 I will not work for Free	10 I will not work beyond 6:30 pm
	2 I will not travel on Sundays	5 I will not eat a heavy dinner	8 I will not do things that can delegate...	11 I will not eat deep fried foods
	3 I will not Work on Sundays	6 I will not watch late-night movies on my working days	9 I will not use more than 2 credit cards	12 I will not buy unnecessary technology

Who needs to do what by when to get the not-to-do list in action?	Staff needs to do more	Staff has a system of evaluation of opportunities	Outsource some of the work to Elance, Guru	Curtail, Delegate, Eliminate what I am not best at:
	I need to take on less	Everyone works what they do best	Sleep early and wake up early	Stop Seminars and do workshops
	Work only on fee based customers	I need to Hire more staff	Stop thinking credit cards as your money	Stop drinking soda

83

I understand that sometimes even when we have our To-do now lists, Too- do-later lists, we wake up and don't feel like doing anything. There's a key to not falling into this pit. The key is how you begin determines how you end. So, if you begin right, you end right.

How you start your day, determines what the rest of your day will be like. So, the goal is to win in the first 1 hour to 3 hours of the day, and this will set you up for winning the rest of the day. The key to winning in the first three hours of the day is to understand how you charge your batteries for the day

What activities would you want to do in the first three hours of the day that will make you feel you have already conquered your day?

_____
_____
_____
_____
_____
_____

Everyone has their customized way on how to get charged. I will share my ad you can use that if that works for you or create your own:

4:45 AM Wake up and Meditate
5:00 AM Exercise
6:00 AM 90-Minute Work- This is where I focus on two big victories for the day and all long-term actions and decisions that bring traction.
7:30 AM Delegation of work and outcomes for the team for the day.
8:00 AM – Get ready to start the day.

The best way to start your day is to meditate for a few minutes on how you want the rest of the day to be. You should have a place where you can access your plan for the day or a list of projects you can choose from when you start the day. I have a temple in my home where I can sit quietly and meditate. Working on projects early in the morning can help you capture victories throughout the day.

The next zone of the day is the pro-active zone where you only focus on the victories that you want to achieve for the day. My cut-off time for the pro-active zone is 1:30 PM and then I move to the coping Zone.

The coping zone is where you give time to react to elements that you need for the day. The day never goes as planned so be ready for unexpected occurrences that can occur throughout the day. You should have at least Plan A-D ready in your mind or stored somewhere easily accessible to be deployed at a moment's notice. These unexpected occurrences may put a damp on your flow. You need to understand that you don't have to react to everything that happens throughout the day. Half of the day is divided between reacting to the day and being disconnected.

What is your Plan A-D for dealing with unexpected occurrences throughout the day?

A. _____
   _____
   _____
B. _____
   _____
   _____
C. _____
   _____
   _____
D. _____
   _____
   _____

If you are stuck on how to plan for unexpected occurrences, please understand that many of these unexpected events or situations are already happening routinely in your life so they are not unexpected. For example, you may be called routinely for information that can be easily found if your team or employees looked for it. Because you have been responsive and sharing information, they have the habit to ask you quickly rather than looking for it. Some of these habits have been built in your team because you have permitted them to build them. It may also require you to initially put some time and preparing a detailed outline of a project before handing it over to someone else. I spend 2-3 hours in building project outlines before handing them over and it saves 100 or more hours in back-end in back-and-forth communications and explanations. The front-end time spent in building project outlines and details is well worth it.

You can also ask yourself the questions below to deal with unexpected situations or events:

•Is this something that I absolutely must attend to at this moment?
•Why did this happen? Or what caused or triggered this to happen?
•Knowing what I know now, what could I have done differently to prevent this from happening again?
•Who needs to do what and by when?

Another technique that works very well is shared by Stephen Covey as part of his "7 Habits of Highly Effective People"[2] and video below:
https://youtu.be/zV3gMTOEWt8

The questions and notes below are a result of the same and my interpretation and application of the concept to help you build what is being described in the video.

When you plan your day, you should know how to allocate different times for your activities. For example, you should know big rocks, small rocks, and sand in your life. And be able to classify them as such so you can accomplish a lot in the day.

Let's start with the Big Rocks. Big rocks in your life are your non-negotiable goals, things that fulfill you, things that you can do to make your business more successful, and things that you can do to make this world a happier and healthier place for yourself and others

What are the big rocks in your life and business based on the goals you set in Book 1 of this series?

List 1- 5 big rocks in your life that needs to be part of your everyday routine.

1._____

_____

2._____

_____

3._____

_____

4._____

_____

5._____

_____

Now let's move on to the small rocks. The small rocks in your life are the things that you love to do but they are not moving the needle in a big way in your business or life but something you have on your bucket list. For example, taking piano lessons or dance lessons.

What are the small rocks in your life and business based on the goals you set in Book 1 of this series?

_____

_____

_____

_____

_____

_____

_____

List 1- 5 small rocks in your life that needs to be part of your everyday routine.

1._____

_____

2._____

_____

3._____

_____

4._____

_____

5._____

_____

Now, let's move to the sand that finds its way between the big rocks and the small rocks. Sand is your mundane day-to-day tasks. For example, replying to emails, text messages, social media messages, surfing, grocery shopping, errands, etc.

What are the "sand activities" that you currently do in your life that take up quite a bit of your time throughout the day?

_____

_____

_____

_____

_____

_____

_____

_____

List 1- 5 "Sand activities" in your life and business that needs to be min-imized and done in between the transition from big rock to sand rock with a certain time limit to the transition.

1._____

_____

2._____

_____

3._____

_____

4._____

_____

5._____

_____

Now we move to the big "Time-Saver" – the one that knocks off so many hours of your day or week in a big way. You have often heard the saying- "my plate is full and has no more room to add" or you may have said that to someone. Multiplication happens by subtraction. If your plate is full, you can have two more plates- "The he or she will do it plate" and the "I'll manage it plate"- Transfer stuff from what's on my plate to the two other plates to free up 15 or more hours per week.

I will attach "the Plate off-loader" tool and show you how you can transfer from your plate to other plates. To make your plate for the day easy to manage.

The "Plate Off-Loader Tool" is a three-part tool. The first one is the "What's on My Plate"? In this tool, you will list out activities or tasks you currently do. You can use this tool for personal as well as business. If you want to do both, I would do them separately so they each are focused.

Also, there is a list of strategies that I have listed in the "What's on My Plate"? tool. You can use it or modify it to suit your needs.

The next part of the plate off-loader tool is "The he or she will do it plate" this plate contains all the responsibilities or outcomes that you would like to delegate to someone. This someone should be a capable and responsible person that you can trust to deliver on the delegated tasks.

The third part of the plate off-loader is the "I'll manage it plate" this contains outcomes or responsibilities that you will manage but not do. However, you need to set a reporting strategy for this. When you do, those who do these tasks can report to you. This is called reporting to management, and it is defined as reporting to management in an organized method of providing each manager with all the data he or she needs to make the right decisions.

I have my quote- "What gets measured and reported takes improvement to a new level"

Please utilize the tools provided on the next pages to free up 15 or more hours weekly. Your intent is at a minimum free up 15 hours a week.

The Plate Off-Loader ™				Name:_____ Start Date:_____ End Date:_____ Job Title:_____
WHAT'S ON MY PLATE? (Be as specific and Detailed as you can to the activities, responsibilities, and outcomes that you do on a curring basis. Please include personal activities or tasks as well if you would like to)	**Average Time**	**No. Times Repeated Weekly**	**Total Weekly Time Taken**	Circle Love it, Like it, Hate it or Can't (P.T.O for Strategies) (In Excel just delete the icons not applicable)
				♥ 👍👎 ?
				♥ 👍👎 ?
				♥ 👍👎 ?
				♥ 👍👎 ?
				♥ 👍👎 ?
				♥ 👍👎 ?
				♥ 👍👎 ?
				♥ 👍👎 ?
				♥ 👍👎 ?
				♥ 👍👎 ?
				♥ 👍👎 ?
				♥ 👍👎 ?
				♥ 👍👎 ?
				♥ 👍👎 ?
				♥ 👍👎 ?
				♥ 👍👎 ?
				♥ 👍👎 ?
				♥ 👍👎 ?
				♥ 👍👎 ?
				♥ 👍👎 ?
				♥ 👍👎 ?
				♥ 👍👎 ?

	Your Strategies
	(Below is a short list to use. You can also create your own)
♥	Make it my Most Valuable Activity
♥	Make it my Long Term Driver
♥	Make it an Activity that Relieves Stress
♥	Make it a Big Rock
♥	Make it an Activity that makes me irreplacable
♥	Make it an Activity that gets me fully charged for the Day.
♥	Activity you need to improve upon
♥	Make your important activities your Critical Activities.
👍👎	Delegate it to the Team
👍👎	Delegate it to a Technology System
👍👎	Delegate to AI
👍👎	Eliminate it through a better technology, Solution, or Process
👍👎	Curtail or Do less of it, until you figure out how to delegate or eliminate
👍👎	Assign to Someone else in the team
👍👎	Eliminate it altogether
👍👎	A habit that you need to change
👍👎	Make it your small rocks or Sands for the Day.
👍👎	Create a process or system for urgent and important activities
👍👎	Is it a Behavior that creates an unwanted domino effect?
👍👎	If it's a activity that you want to love it, block some time to learn and improve it.
?	Curtail it, Delegate it, or Eliminate it through many of the strategies described above
?	Reach to experts outside your organization who have already figured out"how to" in the area that you are stuck
?	Get Training and Research or what you need to learn to master that activity- if you still love to do it
?	Bring it to the attention of people who can help you master this activity, if you still love it

The Plate Off-Loader ™-				Name:_____
The 1st Empty Plate				Start Date:_____End Date:_____
				Job Title:_____

The He or She will Do It Plate (Responsibilities, Outcomes, Tasks or Outcomes you want to delegate to someone)	Who to delegate	How often to be done? (Daily, Weekly, Monthly..etc.)	Total Time FREED UP	What will be the best utilization of that free time?

The Plate Off-Loader ™- The 2nd Empty Plate			
Name:_____ Start Date:_____ End Date:_____ Job Title:_____			
The "I Will Manage it Plate" (Responsibilities, Outcomes, Tasks, or Outcomes you will manage but <u>not DO</u>)	What Reporting System will you use to manage this and how often it is due?	Total Time FREED UP	What will be the best utilization of that free time?

Please take your time to do all the activities given in this chapter, as they will help you manage your time and day. And make sure you're productive.

Congratulations on completing week four, where you learned about making freedom of time, and allowing you to do important things for the growth of your business. Hopefully, you have freed up more than 15 hours of your time every week. You have completed all the stages in this book and are now ready to make the biggest 90-day leap in your business. The next book is just about that!

Before you move on to the next book in the series, please take some time to check out the useful FREE tools and resources and take some time to celebrate your big accomplishment of freeing up 15 hours weekly!!

Week 4

Your Chapter Takeaways

What are the top 10 ways you will free up 15 hours or more weekly?

1._____

2._____

3._____

4._____

5._____

6._____

7._____

8._____

9._____

10._____

What key decisions, habits, and routines do you need to make for those above 10 strategies to be successful?

_____

_____

_____

_____

Useful Resources

QR Code to scan and get all FREE Tools and Resources:

Link from the QR Code:

https://linktr.ee/TheOneYearBreakthrough

Link to all my events:

https://www.eventbrite.com/o/bimal-shah-7943115300

Time to Celebrate

Before you move to the hidden insights, take time to celebrate.

Here are five little ways you can celebrate:

1. 15-hour enjoyment plan with your family.
2. Take the 15 hours you saved up and how much money you saved by freeing up that time and spend 10 percent of that for your spouse.
3. 15 x 4=60 and that means a week of free time over a month- Book a one-week cruise for you and your family.
4. Commit to your family that you are going to make that 15 hours of freedom a reality and you will achieve that by a deadline, and you will go for a three-day vacation with your family- Announce it.
5. Go out and have a nice drink with your best friend who drives you.

Doubling Your Business and Taking Over Your Industry in a Year!
Hidden Insights from this Book

Below, I have provided proven uncharted bottom-line insights from this book to double your business and rise in your industry in a year:

1. *The Strengths-Confidence Loop:*
Remember the Acronym "LOG-BYTE" for the seven stages of the 7 Cs to confidence. The way it would work is you would place each of these alphabets next to "C" to remember. CL stands for Clarity. CO- Commitment. CG- Courage. CB- Capabilities. CY- Consistency. CT- Competent. CE- Confidence.

2. *The WMD System:*
A WMD system you can use every time you feel down or unhappy is to accept that your weakness is thinking that everything is "happening for you" rather than to you. When you believe that, you can move to management of the HOW or WHO and the minor components. You can easily DISCHARGE it with your accountability system.

3. *The Lever and The Fulcrum:*
Choose your World with an eye for the minimum viable but highest quality audience instead of the biggest audience. This will allow you to easily build the strongest and longest lever with the least amount of resources and place it on the right fulcrum that you can do.

4. *Making Freedom of Time.*
The fastest way to get to the goal of freeing up 15 or more hours per week is to allocate an hourly pay to your time by the number of gross revenues you are responsible for bringing into the business. Anything under that, you want to systematize, eliminate, delegate, curtail, or do in less time.

DON'T FORGET

Join The Pioneers Club for FREE!

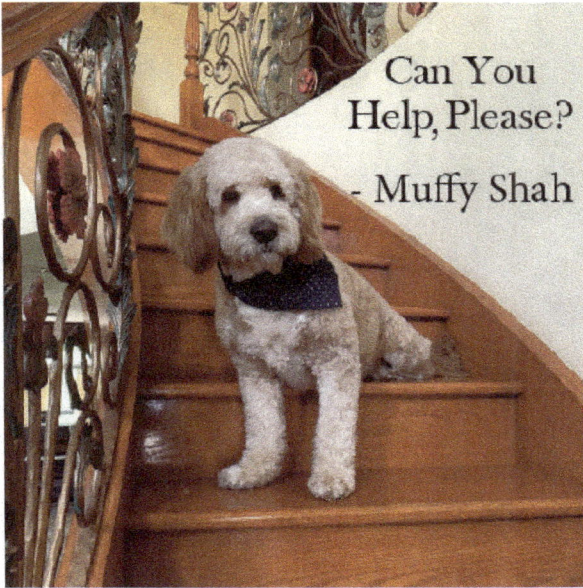

Can You Help, Please?

- Muffy Shah

Thank You for Reading My Book!

I appreciate your reading this book!

I would love it if you can give me an honest review.

I need your input to make the next version and my future books better.

Please leave me a helpful 5-Star review on Amazon, letting me know what do you think?

Thank you so much!
—Bimal Shah

Please don't forget to check out the next book—on making the biggest 90-Day leap in your life and business.

This is the next step in the sequence of steps to Becoming a Pioneer by achieving your three-year goal in one year.

See you in book 6!

DON'T FORGET

Join The Pioneers Club for FREE!

WHAT IS THE PIONEER CLUB FOR A BUCK?

- Buy the book for a Buck and you join the club
- Meet and network with other Pioneers
- Walk away with great results at the club meeting
- Complete the exercises in the book
- FREE Tools and Resources
- Win an Invitation to the Mastermind ($495 Value)
- Provide a great review on Amazon

https://bit.ly/ThePioneersClub

With the purchase of each book, you are Eligible to Join the Club Meeting for FREE

Connect with Pioneers around the World—Every Month. With the book purchase, you are a member. No strings attached.

Connect with Me and walk away with personalized insights for you in the Club meetings held every month on Wednesdays at 6 PM EST.

Walk away with a customized 30-Day Action Plan at each meeting.

Get Your FREE Membership at: https://bit.ly/ThePioneersClub

Conclusion

My dear friend and fellow entrepreneur we have come to the end of this book. It's been an amazing ride. This book if used appropriately will help you leverage your strengths and manage your weaknesses in every area of your life.

The book asks deep questions that call for transformative self-reflection. Please take your time to go through the questions and perform the exercises in each chapter. As they will help you improve greatly in all aspects of your life including your business.

I believe that I have given you everything I can to help you strengthen your strengths and manage your weaknesses so you can succeed in all ramifications.

Bye for now. Can't wait to see you in book six to make the biggest 90-day leap in your life and business.

About the Author

Bimal Shah is an accomplished Senior Executive, Entrepreneur, Advisor, Coach, and Results Leader with more than twenty years of success in the financial services industry. Leveraging extensive experience in growth, entrepreneurship, talent development, financial reporting systems, profitability systems, and processes to scale, he is an asset for companies spanning various industries, sizes, and stages of growth that are seeking expert assistance in bringing their business to the next level. His broad areas of expertise include executive coaching, strategic planning, operations management, scaling, and growth.

As a breakthrough coach, Bimal has successfully helped companies generate growth of more than 50 percent in a year and has taken twenty-six companies to exponential growth in a year. Through his unique hiring process technique, he has helped dozens of companies hire highly qualified C-Level employees. He has worked with more than fifty companies, providing coaching and financial consulting services across an array of industries, including manufacturing, distribution, home health care, communications, security systems, and professional services. His unique Coaching-Planning-Accountability system has generated favorable results in record time for CEOs, reducing their working hours, in six months, by 35 percent.

As a result, CEOs see exponential company growth within a year, can hire smart and productive team members at all levels within a few months, and receive the tools to develop effective "out of the box" marketing strategies.

Bimal is also the founder of Rajparth Advisory Group (2005), which provides financial consulting services to entrepreneurs. From 1996 to 2005, before founding Rajparth Group, he worked as an independent advisor through Northwestern and New York Life, helping more than 1000 families preserve their assets, reduce their taxes, increase their income, and create everlasting legacies.

During his tenure, he was awarded the highest honor in the industry, The Million Dollar Round Table—Top of the Table Award for six years in a row, and Global Corporate Award for Best Life Insurance Agent in the Asian Indian Community.

Bimal has also authored and published *The Daily Happiness Multiplier*, available on Amazon and in bookstores throughout North America. His unique "Success Deck" consists of 52 Workshop Videos and Tools to positively impact anyone's personal and professional life with a single tool each week for 52 weeks. Bimal earned his Bachelor of Commerce in Economics from the University of Mumbai and his Bachelor of Science in Advertising from the University of Florida. He holds a Chartered Financial Consultant, Chartered Life Underwriter, and Certified Advisor in Senior Living from the American College at Bryn Mawr, Pennsylvania.

Some Accolades for Bimal's Work

"Bimal is the big picture guy, and he takes us deep. I might concentrate on one idea that I think is the greatest idea in this world, and Bimal will come back with making us think 10 times bigger and he's got this amazing ability to see opportunity. He lays out a great plan to get to where you want to go and makes it just so attainable. Every entrepreneur with big goals should consider hiring Bimal and if I could have Bimal in my pocket and carry him around always that would be great."
—*Mike Barnhill, Managing Partner, Specialist ID*

"Before, I was working 70–80 hours a week. Now it is down to 45–55 hours a week. The personal impact of his coaching has allowed me to spend more time with my family. The financial impact has been priceless because of the time saved. If you are struggling, consider hiring Bimal. His books and coaching have helped me plan and organize where I want the business to go. Bimal has also taught me to push my limits and think about things more in detail on why I am doing this."
—*Reginald Andre, CEO, Ark Solvers, Inc.*

"Bimal's books and workshops have further reinforced and enhanced some aspects of my leadership; in that, he has brought on a fresh perspective on my role as a leader of the company. In addition to Bimal being a very engaging and energetic personality, he also has an open-minded and unique perspective to making learning a fun-filled experience for my staff, which then adds immeasurable value to my company."
—*Terry Sgamatto, Managing Regional Director, Seeman Holtz*

"I recently took a leap of faith . . . one that required a consistent amount of convincing myself out of a scarcity mindset and making an investment. It has just been a few weeks and I am very happy with the results of my decision. Under the advisement of Bimal, I have had to make some drastic decisions in my company but have to say overall, even though some were painful, they have all been results-driven and not emotional. I truly appreciate all that Bimal has helped me create in the first few weeks and cannot wait to see what comes next."
—*Sarah Martin, CEO, Experience Epic, LLC*

"We hired Bimal to get our company better organized and have better business practices and we have been practicing that every year for so many years now. Bimal is a pretty persistent guy, and he doesn't let us get away with being lazy. He pushed us to accomplish the goals we had set to accomplish—you helped us get it done and he didn't let us be lazy at all. If you want to build a self-managing company, Bimal is the guy-- it's worth the effort and time and it's worth the energy that you are going to put into it as you are going to get every bit and more out of it and the amount of money you spent is insignificant compared to the results you have attained. "
---*Shawn Crow, CEO, Austen Enterprises, Inc.*

"Bimal's coaching and consulting have been very results driven and helped us achieve the milestones we set in taking our company to the next level. Bimal's unique ability to understand our issues and solve the problems is amazing and something that no one else does. For anyone considering working with or hiring Bimal for any of his services, I would recommend they do it without any hesitation or doubt. The results and value far outweigh the investment."
-*Jorge Zuluaga, CEO, First Class Parking Systems, LLC*

Notes

1. "Albert Einstein Quotes." BrainyQuote.com. Brainy Media Inc, 2023. 29 January 2023. https://www.brainyquote.com/quotes/albert_einstein_383803

2. Big Rocks, Small Rocks, Pebbles Time Management System- Stephen Covey's 7 Habits, Stephen Covey- First Things First. Also how President Dwight D. Eisenhower organized his time- Franklin Covey Institute- January 25. 2023.